ANTHONY HOWELL · SILENT HIGHWAY

By Anthony Howell

POETRY

Inside the Castle 1969
Femina Deserta 1972
Oslo: a Tantric Ode 1975
Notions of a Mirror 1983
Why I May Never See the Walls of China 1986
Howell's Law 1990
First Time in Japan 1995
Sonnets 1999
Selected Poems 2000
Spending 2000
Dancers in Daylight 2003
The Ogre's Wife 2009

VERSIONS

Imruil 1970
Statius: Silvae (*with Bill Shepherd*) 2007
Plague Lands (*versions of Fawzi Karim*) 2011

FICTION

In the Company of Others 1986
Oblivion 2002

PROSE

The Analysis of Performance Art 1999
Serbian Sturgeon 2000

AS EDITOR

Near Calvary: The Selected Poems of Nicholas Lafitte 1992

ANTHONY HOWELL
Silent Highway

ANVIL PRESS POETRY

Published in 2014
by Anvil Press Poetry Ltd
Neptune House 70 Royal Hill London SE10 8RF
www.anvilpresspoetry.com

ISBN 978 0 85646 452 2

This book is published
with financial assistance from
Arts Council England

Designed and set in Monotype Bulmer by Anvil
Printed and bound in Great Britain
by Hobbs the Printers Ltd

ACKNOWLEDGEMENTS

'Somewhere Something', 'Tristeza' and 'Grumarí' were first published
in *The Spectator*. 'Ode to the Sunset' and 'Innisfree' appeared in *Ambit*.
'Timing' and 'Final Sunset' came out in *Poetry Salzburg Review*.
'Aging' appeared in *The Babylonian World* edited by G. Leick
(Routledge) 'Orchid' was streamed on *Grey Suit*.

Contents

4   Beachcomber

1

Lord of Storms

Somewhere Something

Rises, as a bowl rises
On a potter's wheel, as a turning bowl
Is raised from the wheel
By fingers inwardly kneading,

Turning a bowl raised by fingers
Turning, twirling onwardly
The whorl of a shell
Revolving, twirling,

Rising, as the shell spirals
On its spindle's shaft, as a turning shell
Revolves through each whorl,
Its spiral upwardly twirling,

Turning the shaft of a spindle,
Twirling, turning outwardly
The bowl on a wheel
That rises, turning,

Rises, as a bowl rises
On a potter's wheel, as a turning bowl
Is raised from the wheel
By fingers inwardly kneading.

Innisfree

When all my mum remembered
Was the isle of Innisfree,
I put her in an old folk's home
And sometimes went for tea.

She couldn't clean herself by then,
She couldn't use the loo.
She only stroked her little dog
And asked me who was who.

I never sat with her for long.
I wanted to be free:
Dress up smart and head for town
To meet with Kerry-Lee.

Now Kerry-Lee wrote poetry:
Her poetry was fine.
I took her to a restaurant
And asked her to be mine.

She said, "Though I'm from Canada,
I've lived for six long years
Up the valleys with a guy
Who never changed his gears.

I'm not prepared to settle down
With anyone just yet."
She smiled the loveliest of smiles
And rolled a cigarette.

"Then sleep with me, at least," I sighed,
"For money, if you like."
So every Friday, after that
She'd visit on her bike.

You could say I was mad for her.
Neglecting my old mum,
I'd lie abed with Kerry-Lee,
While she got through the rum.

With Christmas over, mum took ill
And died within a week.
I drove up to the hospital
And kissed an icy cheek.

Before the crematorium
Had turned mum into ash,
Kerry-Lee had let me know
She didn't need the cash.

Mad for Paul, she was, you see;
My colleague, where I taught.
Then everything got swallowed up
In one enormous nought.

And there being nothing I could do
About my mother's dog,
I left her in the old folk's home
Where things turn into fog.

The Castaway

Our gangling palms bend out towards the sea;
A sea forever bowling in across
The hidden reef where white caps briefly toss.

David's board's by the rail there, freshly waxed,
But since he's seeing Eleanor again tonight
He rolls away, striated by the light.

Our veranda steps are rather steep:
Best to take them sideways, step by step.
Fourteen days ago, she phoned him up.

Off he drove, his board snapped to the rack;
Told me not to worry, he'd be back.
All afternoon they looped the bluest tubes.

The beach bends round our own blue bay. I tread
Where palm tops bash together overhead.
Sand-whipped breezes here can really sting

And a rip will drag you down as swift as anything
And now she's back on the island, just as slim
As ever, and still able to keep up with him.

Poor David, it's unfair to make him choose.
How about me slipping off these shoes
To wade out, overburdened as I am?

Scrabble

"Maybe it was just one skiing holiday too many."
So an article on an artist once well-known
Analysed his slow descent from favour:
Going off piste, through laden pines, into mist.

Bugger all deflects achievers – bent on their careers,
Balanced on the top rungs of ladders
To adjust the height of their stars. A work-out
Takes precedence over conjugal endeavours:

Their legs are insured for too much to venture on hikes.
These are the monsters who matter.
They make history – albeit one full of pratfalls –
One can be famously wrong, unlucky, naive, disliked.

Most of us though are just too immersed in our lives;
Up to our ears in arrears; pulled over
Somewhere *sans* import to answer the mobile
Forever – overwhelmed by duties or desires.

Queuing up at one counter after another,
We hardly advance – too busy heeling our shoes.
We just get to movies or laundries, fit in a swim or a chat,
And garner the letters that spell out *insignificance*.

At least we ought to be able to paint on Sundays.
But Sunday tends to evaporate. It's too much of a wrench
To move from the chair as the afternoon deepens.
Love took its toll in the morning, and then there was lunch.

The Glider

We live for certain moments of intensity:
Spring thickening into impenetrability;
Squirrel babies nipping in and out,

Improving their tails, projecting their images
Onto rosy futures – unlike lemmings.
Heading down a slope towards a cliff,

You suddenly think of something inappropriate,
Utterly so – everyday angels, for instance,
With mobiles and e-mails – and how

They are not really as recondite as you make out.
Indeed the only thing unusual about them
Is that repetitive dream they keep having.

Barring this, the darlings aren't mysterious at all,
And you shouldn't think of them as fetishised
Automatons either – who keep getting run over.

Best appreciate their non-technological reality.
Neither texts, leather-bound, nor bodices
With steel armatures, their appearance

Is not what matters, curiously enough.
You try to penetrate the soul, get inside
Each of them, before you run off the edge.

Rival

Whereas she's no great burden to my bed,
Her visitor should be assigned the floor.
He teases, as she never ever would,
With irritating tugs at the extension.

Nicely, she respects the need for exits,
Leaving my door into the weeds ajar,
And, being something of a Thespian herself,
Appreciates my more dramatic entrances.

Mornings, she's responsive to the prayer,
Opening the altar to secure for me
Libations worth the lowering of hauteur.
Just as a nutriment stales she changes the flavour.

Has the most brushable calves, I declare,
Although I'm rather partial to his trouser.
Never knowingly shall I sink myself unsheathed
Into her contour. There are times, alas,

One suffers from unconscious fits of tenderness,
And nothing's to be done, one has to tread
The memory still soft beneath the paw.
Of course I maul that maul-provoking visitor

Mewling his resentment of the ardour
Lavished upon me by her. She has a use
For him, it seems, although it's clear
That in her breast my tenure's ever paramount.

Timing

It must have been frustrating. They had completed the temple
Ahead of schedule – well almost, to be exact.
The timbers had been prepared, and were stacked
At the back, above the ravine.

The citizens, though, still banked on their masons
Adjusting the fee for a last row of niches;
Their carpenters contracted, and impatient
To get the roof on once this was incised…

The edifice already looked a proper wonder of the world.
It could be seen from the amphitheatre and from the agora.
Admired by all visiting dignitaries, its columns
Filled tall vases with the sky: their shadows combed

The sacred ground, and you could almost savour
The sacrifice soon to be grilled on the altar.
Here was a city practically at the acme of its powers;
Playing off Athens and Carthage, to confound each neighbour.

But this was when Agathocles arrived
With his perfect brain-wave for the roof-beams they would raise –
Turned them into catapults and fired
Eight thousand citizens into the ravine.

Mind you, it took him three days …

Epitaph

Philocrates had a friendly dog
And a bright whirligig.
At five, he died,
But it had been worth it.

Physis

Jack, the strong octopus,
With more arms than a company,
Embraces with his trades
The ideal of metamorphosis.

Nataraja, dancing the Tandara
On the demon of ignorance,
Is the transformer, the storm,
His tentacles muscular,

Their tips accurate,
And delicate – expressive,
With a finger to a pie.
Now I know nought whatsoever,

But to walk through her
As she walks through me
Arouses the drum, the cobra,
The flame and the gesture.

My love is my weight:
Where it goes I go.

Birth of the Dance

Their intercourse, if fruitful, would create
A demon charged with unquenchable heat;
The product of their cosmic powers combined.

On plunging into the deep, this ogre troll
Might well give rise to a flood that would never
Evaporate. All they could do for a celestial

Aeon or two was re-entwine in tantric ways:
Torture for these mutual devotees –
Doomed to go at it as pestle and mortar

Grinding some recalcitrant root of the forest's
Wiry Soma. Again and again he reached
The brink only to hold back, to think

Of spinach or the horrible teeth of the gate-keeper.
Finally the one ground the other down:
When all had worn away, the dance was born.

Lord of Storms

Back from the coast, on a breezy hill, there's a heaving
In the dense bamboo, and an undertow
Of rustle from those cataracts of morning glory
Burgeoning, since a god split a serpent in two,
By the spring that used to serve the aqueduct.

Vritra had sucked up every last drop, so we must thank
Lord Indra for the water which now spills
Out of our plunge pool, causing this profusion
That overwhelms the view: as easy to get lost in it
As it is to get lost in a poem – a growing tract

Of jungle spilling down a cleft hewn between deserts
By little more than a ditch. Bamboo, great walls of bamboo.
Beyond its palisades, solar panels follow the sunflower's lead.
A field of shields, a field of blackened disks.
Now the morning glory furls. Darkness falls in mauve

And blue. We look into the pupil of the night,
And daylight's blooms deepen into tones of resonance ...
The purple under your eyes, the whirlpools
Of unhurried time widening into stillness,
Repeating, ever more slowly, the ghost of a meaning.

Doesn't it flow at different rates in different parts
Of the cosmos? Now there's the hoot of an owl
And sombre shades start bleeding into the dream's aromas.
Being Indandra by name, they call him Indra cryptically.
For the *devas* love the cryptic, yea, they love the cryptic.

Kaliyuga

From the prose of David Stacton

For the goddess it is easier.
As she grows older, she gains in authority
And becomes a matriarch.
The god without a cheque-book
Knows himself supplanted, and a fool.

The goddess is a dynasty: but the god
Is just an enfeebled King of the Wood
Tottering along the shores of Lake Nemi,
Waiting for the gladiator
Caesar has forgotten to dispatch.

An immortal cannot pass away,
But may be left unfêted by his followers.
The older he gets, the younger he feels,
And the greener his apsaras
Needs to be; not woman, but symbol.

KALIYUGA: *the "age of vice" is the last of the four stages that the world goes through as part of the cycle of yugas described in the Indian scriptures.*

APSARAS: *a female spirit of the trees – a dryad.*

Aging

Euphrates, your boulevards,
Palmyra, your bazaars!
Pillars, columns, foresting the waste.
High facades, hidden
From the living now
By smoke, fire, the hot breath of the Gods.

I sit, today, underneath the clouds:
Each has a calmness of its own.
I sit, today, underneath the oaks:
Each has a grandeur of its own.
Deer feed nearby. The doings of exalted ones
Fill me with little but indifference.

After Hölderlin

2
Silent Highway

Silent Highway

1. *Heraclitus*

Apotheosis! Arsenals of the sky
Ablaze, exploding, crimsoning the crowns
Of storm clouds over Woolwich with its furnaces
Producing the great barrels of our guns.
Apotheosis, mist-suffused at sunrise
As the duck wing over Dagenham Breach.
Those decent acres have been overwhelmed
By the sky's double, Father Thames,
The Tiber's brother, leaning on his couch
Of bales and bundles, ever outward bound;
His oar is more a cricket-bat, his ewer
Overflows with tributes such as Isis
Brings to bless his bridges and his Pool.
Her masons swear by Cleopatra's needle.
There she dances with her timbrelled maids –
As high on chants as any Hari Krishna.

Apotheosis, Phoebus in his car,
Driving away demonic clouds with deafening
Percussion in the vanguard of their flashes,
Just like Alice scattering the cards
To call a halt to rolling heads,
While William and Mary ascending
Get as far as that wide ceiling there
In the painted Hall of Greenwich where
We chorus, Tyranny avaunt!

Avaunt, ye darksome powers, most inglorious!
Unconstitutional monarchies, rights divine!
Now let's be enlightened, leave a space
Between the buildings for the Queen
To get a view of Canary Wharf,
Sir Christopher, no wider than her house is.

*   *   *

Heraclitus knew about rivers,
Knew that in differing, banks agree,
Talked of a backward-turning connection,
Like that of a bow or a lyre.
You could say the path of a river
Is both straight and crooked at once,
Since the water flows in one direction
While each bend conducts it in another.
Thus it is the Thames wends north at Westminster,
Thus it is it swings due east at Southwark:
Impulses reversed though, as the tide comes in.
The path either way is one and the same,
For we are all flowing through time.
The river is day and night, winter and summer,
War, peace, youth and old age.
It quenches the sun, and it sets the moon
Ablaze with its rippling dance.
Into the selfsame river
No one can ever step twice,
For dropsical Heraclitus knew

That the universe flows like a river
And that the river is fire.
Think of the Great Fire of London
Sweeping across old London Bridge,
Heating the starlings, the cut-waters,
Warming the current, or think of Rum Quay
On fire in the blitz: a river of flame.
A river is like a book, you can get lost
In it – as it was said of the book
Of Heraclitus, it would take a Delian
Not to drown in it.

*   *   *

The Thames is rising fast
While you play me without haste
At a game I'm meant to lose,
Though you end up in my shoes
And tell me we might stay
Together, were we free.

And why should you be lying?
You move beneath me sighing
At the high tide of our dream,
While the river flows upstream
To flood the reach profusely
As you spread about me loosely.

But how we are just now
We both of us well know
Isn't easily surpassed
So it better be the last,
For love will surely start
To tear our lives apart.

Then everyone around us
Will hate us and confound us,
For it's only at the neaps
One wades across these deeps;
And now if we go further
We will drown in each other.

2. *Pocahontas*

Thus the river sanctions love and lust
For water, being water, isn't dust;
And sailors like their ladies in less clothes
Than might seem proper – light shifts and bare toes.
Call it, then, a short chemise, or mini-skirt,
That Nannie wears on board the Cutty Sark.
Weird perhaps for a clipper ship
To be christened after a sister of Old Nick:
"But Nannie, far above the rest
Hard upon noble Maggie prest
Whose spring brought off her master hale
But left behind her ain grey tail,
And when to drink you are inclined
Or Cutty-sarks run in your mind,
Think, ye may buy the joys o'er dear,
Remember Tam O'Shanter's mare"
And Nannie's speed, which brought the tea
From China each new season with a tail
Of old rope painted grey within her clutch
When she sailed in past Greenwich with
A stack of well-aired Twankey in her hold.
Think of this silent highway – in its heyday
Anything but silent – silent now;
But not when Pocahontas sailed this way,
On a sparkling morning – cloudless blue,
A light wind helping and a silvery haze
Improving London town. But it was hard
To walk so, in moccasins on cobble-stones:
Hard to be ignored by James the First,

Though he looked fine in the palest blue
On a foaming, fiery horse, and then,
After a nicer interview with dour
Sir Walter Raleigh, feverish, in the tower,
Who knew the doings of the Powhatan,
Hard to die at Gravesend, of consumption,
Within a year, her long anticipation
Heralding so short a stay in London.

*   *   *

Some have come in dread, Sir Henry Morgan
        being but one example, clapped in irons,
Damned to hell, a braggart buccaneer
        heading for the dock and execution,
Only to be dubbed a knight and sent
        back to Jamaica, governor of the island ...

Some have started out from here, aboard
        the vessels built at William Fairbairn's works
At Millwall, in the engineering shops,
        at the joiners, on the pattern-makers' benches,
In the foundries, in the smithies;
        in the yards with every stout appurtenance
For constructing ocean-going tonnage.
        Here were built the *Grappler* and
The *Megaera* for the navy, and
        "the largest vessel floated", the *Great Eastern.*

Iron hulled, the "Eastern" was intended
    to unnerve the sirens of the Cape.
Her length was more than three times that
    of the Monument on Fish Street
While her breadth was equal to Pall Mall's.
    Promenades around her deck
Afforded a walk of a quarter-mile.
    Designed by Isambard Kingdom Brunel,
She boasted a brace of engines, two propellers,
    and her bridge's 'cellular' construction.
She *combined* the might of steam
    by using paddle-wheels *and* screws,
Featured ten boilers, five funnels
    and a hundred furnaces – or more.
Her paddle-wheels were sixty feet in height;
    each one of them some ninety tons in weight.

"A Floating City," so averred Jules Verne:
    and one required to lay the Atlantic cable.
She alone could store its miles of wire.
    and when she afterwards became
A transatlantic liner, her interior
    was fitted out at horrible expenditure.
The ladies saloon and the grand saloon
    were ornaments with lustres,
Lamps and rosy, risqué pictures.
    Skylights lit the dance-floors. Gilded pillars
Framed the stairs whose genuine mahogany
    led baluster by baluster towards the upper deck.

Prospective passengers though took fright
     at the sight of this female Colossus
And so she never prospered, the *Great Eastern*,
     failing at times to answer to her helm,

Maybe her myth would have been the more glorious
     had she gone down, bullies,
Had she gone down.
     But ignominiously, she ended up
Conveying coals from Newcastle to London,
     then was sold for scrap.

*   *   *

"A well-featured but wanton young girl"
Playing in her pre-nubile nakedness
Within the Jamestown settlement:
Leapfrogging, turning cartwheels with the cabin-boys,
Powhatan, her father, chief of chiefs,
A tall and well-proportioned man
With a sour look, his head inclined to grey,
His beard so thin it seems no beard at all.
His warriors, six foot tall, are clad in pelts
Which barely hide their privities;
Live garter-snakes, their ornaments,
The right side of the scalp shaved with a shell,
The left side worn like a knotted tail.
They paint their faces blue or white,

And put on buckskin leggings in the fall.
Their priest totes a snake-skin head-dress
Stuffed with moss, and at their ceremonials,
They dine on tasty maize-cakes, broiled
Fish on hurdles, guinea fowl and venison,
With fresh oysters, baked inside their shells,
As for their entertainment are dismembered
The bodies of their captives piece by piece
While they yet live. The cultivated gentlemen
Of Jamestown, on the other hand
Look especially grand in their Sunday
Satin or taffeta finished with slashes.
They cultivate rich pinking and embroidery
And doff their plumes at the Eucharist
Before they hang the colonist who has missed
The service for three Sundays in succession.

"Bid Pocahontas bring hither
Two little baskets
And I will give her white beads
To make her a chain."

3. Windrush

Into what world, then, came such noble savages,
Or the Huguenots, or the refugees, or the immigrants?
They slid beneath the city, shot the bridge,
A risky business in the time of Pepys.

Then London Bridge was crammed with leaning houses,
Chimneys, water-mills and traitors' heads,
And London's river seemed indeed a pool.
And if they trudged up Watling Street from Dover

Gog and Magog stood guard on London's gate:
The sole survivors of some monstrous brood,
Offspring of the thirty-three hard daughters
Of the Emperor Diocletian. They had murdered

All their husbands; then, being set adrift,
Reached Albion, and there fell in with demons.
Out of their union sprang a race of giants
Seventeen foot high, a plague of freaks

Extirpated by the resourceful Brut.
He only spared Magog and Gog, their leaders.
Led in chains to London, these were taught
To serve as porters at the palace, now

The Guildhall, where their golden-armoured effigies
Have stood at least since the reign of Henry V.
Their oldest figures went up in the blaze
That swept the bridge and burnt out London's plague.

The next ones came down with the blitz, but still
They stand in their most recent incarnation,
Only nine foot high, but looking Roman,
Now *inside* the hall. With civic pride,

They flank musicians in the wooden gallery.
And if you climb the spiral stairs within
Wren's monument, constructed with the cash
Meant for the Great Fire's orphans, for a view

Of Tower Bridge where the warship lies at anchor,
Or look out west towards Saint Paul's or north
Across the city's gleaming glass cathedrals,
Or glance below, at taxis in a jam,

And pleasure boats and launches, tugs and barges
Glimpsed between tall spires, mediaeval buttresses,
Satellite dishes, ventilation apertures,
Then you will sense that Gog and his companion

Still serve London, working now as cranes,
By swinging round prefabricated slabs
Or dropping chains to be attached to canisters
Amid the whine of saws, the clang of metal.

*   *   *

"Sweet Thames, run softly, till me end I song,
Me quit the West Indies and the journey be long.

I daddy fly a Spitfire. He never come back.
I ma, she teach the school, but we living in a shack.

When Mr Clement Attlee be driven by his wife
In a Hillman Minx, we think, this is the life!

When Mr Harold Wilson make a bonfire of Controls
We come to Great Britain to repair their holes.

And when me see the chimneys ranged along the shore
Me say with all them factories no one can be poor.

Though me shiver for the cold on the Tilbury Docks
Me think about the gold to be put into a box.

But they say, if we admit them dammit that'll mean
An ever greater influx of Jamaicans on the scene.

So they grudge we our jobs and they don't let we places,
Because we is we – and they don't wear we faces.

Thing is that they can't make head or tail of how we talk.
Thing is that they don't say good day to we at work.

And if we ride the bus then no one sit beside we,
And they all hide their eye and they rail and they deride we,

And we sleeping in the street, and it hard for we to stick it,
But then me think at least we can beat them at the wicket.

All the sweat of working bc to set things up back home,
But it's more than fifty year, and me still on the roam.

Man, it's just the women here who make we feel alive:
Had I share of them since the day me arrive.

Ain't they lain beside we, the smooth night long?
Sweet Thames, run softly, till me end I song."

                    *   *   *

The canine dead wash up on the Isle of Dogs.
          But under that sheer obelisk of glass there
The docks are like capital letters made of water.
          Water and glass … Madonna's penthouse, Bowie's …

But "back in the 1840's most of London's
          water still came from the Thames,
Polluted by outfall from sewers,
          by stable dung, putrefied sprats and guano,

And by the rubbish and offal thrown into it
          from slaughter-houses, knackers' yards,
Tanneries and tar works. The colour
          was a greeny black, and its consistency so thick

That each time the tide went down
    a greasy, foul-smelling scum was deposited over the mud.
In 1849 the drainage system –
    if so noisome a collection of leaking pipes,

Uncovered cess-pits, stinking gullies,
    rotting privies and gas-filled sewers
Could be called a system at all
    – combined with the shallow, overcrowded

Burial grounds and a pall
    of smoke-filled, disease-ridden fog
To produce a cholera which could kill
    four hundred people a day."

I doubt that this affected the robust
    river pirates, or the night plunderers, or the light horsemen
Or the heavy horsemen who relieved
    the overladen game ships of their strap,

And generally went furnished with habiliments
    designed to hide all manner of commodities:
Sugar, coffee, cocoa and pimento,
    carried on shore by means of an under waistcoat

Harbouring pockets all round, and also
    surreptitious bags, pouches, socks
Tied to their midriffs underneath their trowsers.
    They pilfered there in consort with the game

Watermen whose habit was to place
    the oil-casks upside down in their lighters,
So that the oil could seep out
    and into the false bottoms of their craft.

Then there were the scuffle hunters, good
    at taking advantage of spills and disputes.
Meanwhile, on the water side by Blackfriars,
    clusters of mudlarks might be seen

'At work where the barges were lying.
    They would prowl about at low water
Pretending to grub for old nanny tails, iron:
    boys and girls mostly, from eight to fourteen,

Ragged, in a very filthy state.
    Sometimes they would get between the barges,
And one of them would lift the other up
    to toss the coal-lumps out into the mud,

Coal they would pick up afterwards,
    and sell among the lowest class of people.
And some were old women who would wade
    in the grey mud up to their knees.

One of these might be seen at Wapping,
    her bonnet tied with a handkerchief,
Picking up coals from the river's bed
    and putting them into a bag she had:

Coals she would offer for sale in the town,
    wandering barefoot in an old gown,
        her coal-bag balanced on her head.

4. *Uncle Rufus*

Launched with a huge array of cast-iron ornament,
Notably shields displaying the crest
Of the London, Chatham and Dover Railway Company,
Daubed in heraldic colours but declared
By the public a monstrosity, Blackfriars
Merged with the nearby bridge of Saint Paul's.
The merger brought it pulpits and parapets.
Then on the 15th of June, 1982, four years after
The assassination of a rather decent pope,
The body of Roberto Calvi was found at the end of a rope
Beneath the granite arches of this bridge;
His hands tied behind his back,
His jacket pocket weighed down by a brick.

Blackfriars marks a corner of that square
Mile that keeps the city split off from the town.
Deeply involved in a fraudulent Vatican loan
Which led to the implosion of his banco,
Calvi fled to England carrying a portmanteau
Filled with ambrosial banknotes. Banking on a deal
With Opus Dei, whereby they would acquire a
Holding in his bank by paying off the Mafia,
Calvi was obliged to bankroll Propaganda Due.
Bankrupt – and corrupted by its puppet-master, Gelli –
While frantically attempting to plug the gaping hole
In his bankbooks, he had agreed to launder
The drug engendered profits of the Corleone family.

He never laundered the money though. Instead,
He "borrowed" it to keep his ship afloat.
Opus Dei reasoned that with Calvi dead,
The total collapse of his stocks would result
And this in turn dislodge their powerful
Enemies in the Curia, opening the way for them
To gain total dominance of the Vatican.
It was revealed by a Mafia informer
That Calvi had been strangled by the Mafia's
London based heroin traffic manager.
Bridges are the sacred responsibility
Of the Whitefriars of Paris. But this is the bridge
Of the masons, of the shadowy

Practitioners of corporate piracy, the mighty
Of the mercantile world; those who dictate
That Canary Wharf shall be shaped
Like an obelisk and that its shadow
Shall fall over Hawksmoor's church
With the pyramid beside the gate at Limehouse.
Some say Captain Smith was a mason,
And so was Powhatan, who knew him
By some sign – and this saved Smith,
And it was nothing to do with Pocahontas!
In this reach, on an August night in 1989,
Two hundred young people were partying
Aboard that tidy pleasure boat, the *Marchioness* …

*   *   *

A summer-barge of jollity
Afloat on bags of lolly,
Members of the quality
Took coffee on 'The Folly'.

There the wits would gad about
And squawk like pretty Polly.
Nothing to be sad about
When frequenting 'The Folly'.

The lounge of every wealthy earl
With nothing in his nolly,
As well as Addison and Steele.
How splendid was 'The Folly'.

But where Queen Mary once had trod
Came trollop veiled in trolly,
Many a gambler's curse on God
Was heard aboard 'The Folly'.

Then drapers' smudged apprentices
With city girls most jolly,
After shop was shut and all,
Would sail up to 'The Folly'.

At length the boat grew scandalous
And Amsterdam's plump Molly
Proved the poor man's Tantalus
Below decks, on 'The Folly'.

At last it fell into decay
Abandoned by each dolly.
Sold for firewood, so they say,
The Somerset's old 'Folly'.

*   *   *

Three hundred miles of embankment between
Westminster Bridge and the Nore;
All much improved by the Romans
Who could handle the spade or the spear:
Navvies just as much as soldiers,
Paviours of the world beneath their feet,
Bridge-builders, ferrymen, waders of fords.

Downstream, where the river widens,
Eager to engage the seas it bullied in imperial times –
When "all the liquid world was one extended Thames" –
Monks laid claim to marshland, making fields,
Though Dagenham's fields were overrun
By floods no river wall could quite accommodate;
Old as the turns of its stream, though it be,

With its moorlog of buried yew tree,
Antler, hazel, brushwood, fir …
The stone embankments put in place by Bazalgette
Annoy my uncle, Rufus Noel-Buxton.
He placed the river in chains! he maintains,
Quoting some inscription to the architect.

Uncle Rufus waded the Thames
At Westminster, to prove the Romans did it.
Do you like wading in dark water?
May I invite you to the old Westminster Ford? –
Not just any old ford but the most famous ford in the land.
It took you across the largest river in England.
A ford famous before the Romans
But paved by them along with Watling Street.

Watling Street, the road from the Cinque Ports
To Chester in the far north-west of England,
Tackling the sluggish Thames at Westminster
Just at the point where it was very broad
And pitched against its own intended flow –
'Slowed' by the swings of the river
At Charing Cross and at Pimlico.

Well, do you want to do it? Do you like dark water?
Soaked through, in his galoshes, he spooks
The Upper House, rousing Lords from slumber:
"I only swam two strokes!"
A Labour peer, hereditary, unhappy
That his claim was neither based on merit
Nor on more than a single generation,

Uncle Rufus championed emigration
More or less for everyone except
For ancient Britons, if they could be found,
For bird-watchers, for birds, for water-violets ...

He liked to talk to herons, being tall,
And waded here, and further up, at Brentford
Composing poems as he strode or strove

To stride across each waterway, imagining
Himself a Roman soldier known as Flavius
And getting published by a little Press,
His poem sanctioned by the Poet Laureate
Who did not know much about gods; but
Thought that the river was a strong brown god—
Sullen, untamed and intractable ...

*   *   *

Envoy

For bird-watchers, for birds, for water violets,
You need to get up further, though at Battersea
A cormorant has settled near the house-boats,
Ducks come dabbling by the shore and gulls
Mew back at the squeals of brakes on the bridge.
In autumn swifts will fling themselves skywards
Above the Port authority's "Driftwood" –
A barge employed for mooring other barges
Laden with containers. Past it flow
The sodden newspapers, the spars
Of ancient brooms, the toilet-seats and cans
We have come to expect now of our careless age.
The water is diagonally divided by
The jumbos floating down towards Heathrow.
It's best we leave the river though at Westminster,
For this is where it's at its most rhetorical,
A reliable surge past an insecure seat of government,
Ever on time with its tides, unhurried …
Imagine it as it might have been a century ago,
Just as Monet painted it, envisaging
His indigo impression, twists of cloud,
The water like a nocturne by Debussy,
And flecks of gold transforming tall Big Ben
Into a tower as enchanted as Rapunzel's …

3
Seeing Myself

Orchid

Jet-black roads with ample curves, and like
A low-slung bra-cup, the moon, leaning over
The midlands on the far side of the motorway.
Think of a blank, drowned eye, as in *Les
Diaboliques*, and blink at the oncoming eyes
That roll at you out of darkness, pips ahead

Reflected in the tarmac, as you go coasting
Home, soft on the pedal, dipping at brights:
An elderly hard-up single, heading back from
Some dismal suburb of Peterborough; one
Reflecting still on what was over all too soon
Who takes the slip-road to some windswept

Station, pays through glass, then swings
On without a snack, joins the speeding track,
Headlamps guessing the lane, the returning
Glow of London coming and going in a confusion
Of routes and relationships, this kind arse
Or that, a souvenir on the fingers, half

Ashamed you have to roam thus far to get a lay:
Eighty miles or so from home, risking the flash
Of speed traps at one a.m., the wipers weeping rain.
There was a bleak room to sit till a kid
With just one toy was sent to bed. No holiday,
But then, that giant flower would be worth a crash.

Otter Possibility

How the land sways! Loosestrife and Balsam
Mustered into barricades hiding the marsh scrapes from sight.
Hanging drops in clusters dip as the poplars wave

And weave between the willows' sweeping skirts.
Hawthorne rivals the clouds in white cascades. The land
Is all at sea, for silver birches fret and toss,

Or flail with their branches thrown right back: it's far too wild
For weeping; their leaves obliged to show their undersides.
Down and up, forward and across, the grasses race,

Much like impending breakers. Clouded with leaves,
The trees seem ready to burst. Lincoln, lime
And the yew's deep navy clash, then separate,

Then clash again as a shiver scuds across the glints
And ripples glitter through the rushes' blades.
Only in a pond's armpits does the water coagulate,

Brewing a scum of down, or lurk beneath a duckweed film
Laid like a floor by ivy-fettered brickwork.
Each island soughs as cloud clumps way above

Coast on the accelerating air; islands that may just sustain
The weight of a single pylon; islands rubbing shoulders with
Each other. We move through a stream of stars,

Skirt the prohibited recesses of a private fishery,
Spot an electric demoiselle and pay scant attention to the
    warnings.
We carry no rods, risk no cast so awry as to hook on a cable.

The shadows are dancing too. There is starch in the air.
There are babies everywhere, worrying after their mothers.
A crow alights on the blossom. Everything swishes its

Tail or its tassels. The water goes green then black
Then brown then grey. A gannet stabs and
Comes up with the goods. We are on the lookout

For spraints, for webbed paw-prints, maybe a distant head,
But the sleek one reintroduced here still remains a rarity
Sought for from hides while a bittern *might* boom in the
    reeds ...

Blossom

Beyond little storms in the suburbs
– Cherry confetti, snow-fall from the plums –
There are the stately homes, the manors
With their pastures beckoning cars,
Overdone chambers, third-rate pictures,
Gardens far too pricey to be visited.
Best release their parkland bars
And wander free as airborne seeds

Past chestnut chandeliers.
Perhaps we should make for the folly
Up on the knoll overlooking a lake.
Yes, but the edge of a lake's the spot,
With its reed-fringed, deep
Green grass, to pop a cork. There,
With the scent of a girl's legs in the air,
A hawthorn tenders crowded boughs:

One tree's low hung branch
Improvises as a swing.
The girl upended bicycles the sky,
While a swan with dignity
Contemplates its beak.
Long squeak of a cattle-gate.
Constantly, a light-attracting down
Drifts across the partly ruffled water.

Nepenthes

The only evidence of invisible women,
These anatomical vaginas form themselves
From stalks that have grown out of leaves.
Aberrant blooms that have got it all wrong?

Or are they the next delicious thing –
More alluring than the vampires of Berlin?
Each one a purple vial to drown a rat in,
Patiently ingesting its remains. Time-honoured

Transformation! Protein changed to lush vegetation.
Quintessential females, lidded so as to prevent
Premature exit, who float above their dais of moss.
Urns presented in chorus: a choir of harpies

Making up an exhibit in a tent more sweat-inducing
Than any rain forest. Their low-level chandeliers
Actually remind me of the milking machines
That get attached in parlours. Just as effectively

They squeeze the goodness out of their nutrients.
Clearly their role is to further promiscuous metaphor
Rather than resemble any other plant
On show here at a sweltering Hampton Court.

SLOIPS *

Dense in their entanglement,
The weeds on surplus ground
Stoke up on the missing
Never to be found.

And should you roll to a halt
Beside some sealed-off tract,
You muse about its equivalent
Unmentionable act.

A darker self exists
Whose urges, disinterred,
Propagate like the morning glory
Trumpeting unheard.

* *Surplus Land Overlooked In Planning*

Conservatory

They're fetching with their speckled tongues,
Their lush, ideal mouths, their labia to die for.
One attains perfection here:

Her contours at the crisp
Peak of stellar purity; the sac ripe, striated.
Ah, that absolute

Instant of herself at best,
And next to her a withered one,
The sac a deflated thing.

Edge of Essex

Beyond *The Fish and Eels*, then across the bridge
From Ratty's Lane, a far cry from the hauliers
Surging on up the A10, an indefatigable
Spaniel barks for repetition of retrieval between

Sedge and mustard seed. Where the bank
Breaks off into one small slope of pebbled clay,
He plunges in and paddles out ambitiously
For a coke bottle hurled in the direction of lines

And pylons miniaturised by distance; a mere suggestion
Of power, more or less hidden by willows. The whiff
Of a joint passed round by the barge bohemians
Lounging with their naked knees propped on the bench

Behind us, wafts us, beyond the complicated splash
Of a youth who a second before launched into
Space on his bike, out across the Corot stillness of our
Gravel pit to dream about that wilderness over there

Which glories in a density barricaded by rushes
Backed up by brambles and fundamentally
Impenetrable except perhaps to stoats and foxes:
Green repository of gloom, only its hawthorn

Shimmering. Even so, a stroll this close to an
Industrial zone's obliged to mix the pastoral
With passages more ominous. Back on the broader
River, below fusilli insulators tethering a brace

Of mammoths to their stabilising gantry,
There's a sunken tank that's fenced off from us:
Scum of seeded fluff scurfing up one putrid corner,
Walls of rusted iron making it a cert that

Once you were in you'd be hard pressed to get out.
Possibly it secretes a fair number of weighted
Corpses, but hey, you take the rough with the smooth,
Iris and comfrey perhaps with that scorched patch

And long gone Jack Daniels. It's not on this stretch
That you came across the waterlogged carcass of
A spaniel turning as it drifted down the stream.
For every brutal attack there's a silver lining:

Swimming as flat as you can in the six inches of warm,
Fosters out of the ice-box and some cheap but
Cheerful redhead undeterred from bathing in
Her knickers by the fact they're lacy and transparent.

The Deserted Garage

Cracks have appeared in the concrete and some tough, urbanised
    grasses
Have sprung up. You can't get onto its forecourt with wheels any
    more:
Some circular blocks have been dropped across entrance and exit
While metal roller blinds have been pulled down in front of its
    shop.

Its pumps are hooded, and its car-wash has been dismantled. Gone
Are the twin perpendicular brushes that used to spin as they
    closed in
On your bonnet. Fragments of grimed and mildewed glass
Litter their rusted track. The lavatories are padlocked round the
    back.

However somebody has taken a crow-bar to the Ladies, wrenching
The door off its hinges, and within the sink is intact although
You can't get even a dribble of rusted water out of its single tap,
And both the toilets are seat-less, and one of the bowls has a gap
    in it.

And on the bank to the rear of the site, where there used to be that
    plastic
Goblin tree with the slide in it and the tented rigging for climbing
    up,
There's nothing: the tree has moved on, the rigging has been
    taken down.
Ragwort and thistles encroach now on the grass that once was
    mown.

A newly built by-pass accounts for the drop in volume
     affecting this stretch,
Which is less than congested, these days, restored to its rural
     veneer;
And safe-ish for cyclists, but clearly from the perspective of
     any petroleum
Vendor far from worthwhile, and so there's no longer a
     filling-station here.

What remains is for sale, I guess, but who could possibly
     want it?
Derelict monument to the age of oil, already being
     superseded by sugar-beet
Fuel, wind-power, tidal generators, and doubtless by far more
     inventive
Methods of transport in the future, teleportation, for
     instance, beaming …

Years down the line, the Council will call in the bull-dozers,
     order the JCBs
To break up the forecourt, to knock down the shop, rip up
     the battered pumps
And send them off to the scrap-heap, along with that rusted
     compressor
Lying on one bent and eroded support like some defunct
     grass-hopper

By the debris of the air machine. Then nettles and vetch will
   assemble
And thorn-trees, and maybe the wild plum and certainly thickets
   of bramble
Where thrushes will nest, and small creatures running on smaller
   ones,
While bugs and gastropods will come to inhabit an overgrown
   copse

Here obstructing a view from the road of sink estates and staple
   crops.

Near Clouds Hill

He flew over my bonnet like a super-hero.
I had hoped to circumvent the queue
By making a u-turn. Well, it's down to me,

But they will hog the hump of the road
As if their tires unrolled the line.
Near Bovington, some ten days on,

I just avoid two dawdling boys
On bicycles beyond a rise.
When T. E. Lawrence flew off his

He ended up garrotted by barbed wire.
My father's had a bad rep with its side-car.
He scowls in front of it in uniform,

Then takes off for the Opera or for Paestum
In 1945. I wonder whether those boys
Are alive, or the ghosts of dead bikers?

Tryst in a Suburb

No leaves as yet, this eerie winter of heat.
However, the magnolias are out:
Pale tulip vanes, with lightly tinted blushes
Deepening to amethyst, their petals
Forming goblets on bare branches.

Such flamboyance graces a front garden,
Where they can bare their all to the sun
That's bright today, as I arrive in Morden,
Knowing her only by a snap or two:
Slender, as is shown off by her rump

And frontal view in a twin-set, flimsy, pink;
Kindling my interest in buds that open in secret;
Hyacinths, for instance, their blooms
Giving scent behind curtains, and succulent
Corollas open to accelerated moistening.

The notion of her naked, as if she were wearing
Electricity, defeats my apprehension as
I turn into her street; to find her tall and skinny,
In black leggings and a paint-stained shirt
Doing up a corner of her kitchen.

Lakenheath

It's all top-secret and ever so strictly prohibited.
Making it a cert that this is where
Our heat-seeking darts have their arsenals.
This must be missile mission-control
– Where we go on raids from, with our allies –
It *must* be – where their stealthy wings

Steal into bunker-thick hangers at first light.
You can't stop near its gates, wouldn't
Really want to take a photo, even though
You could tell them you're only a poet
Hoping to get a true-to-life but
Lyrical description of somewhere the size

Of a small county – bristling with hostility;
Fenced-in by razor-wire, shielded
From spooks, from crazies, but with a bright
Blue and red playground for toddlers
Within its compound. Here the sons and daughters
Of the military get to use the jungle gym

Which might be a target elsewhere, since the enemy
Are always doing that, burying weaponry beneath
Their slides and bouncy castles and so on.
Everything's guarded by gimlet binoculars here:
Perhaps we've stashed some gear
Beneath that brightly spotted toadstool fortress.

Fat Romance

Bubbles burst. The whisper of the living
Hints at surreptitious pissers
Hidden pretty slimly by some birches.

Thunder will sour that oblong of water,
Driving off its dragonflies. Now
There's the whoosh of blades, a blur,

As a chopper sent to monitor the orbital
Hangs for a peek. Below it, Miniten
Is played with nothing on except the mitts.

Frayed triangular Union Jacks
Are strung along the roof of a barbeque
Threatened with collapse should bubbles

Happen to smash into it. Deck-chairs
Take the strain of loungers under sun-caps.
Keep your eyes on theirs, or on their gold.

Equally exposed are vales like
Nothing on this earth and oh such folds,
You could drive sheep inside. The breeze

Fluffs up the clouds, the wiry copse,
The sparse, unlikely cabbage-patch,
But carats, twenty-four, one *can* admire:

Chains and watches dripping on ascent
Out of sliding lozenges no Hockney
Need concoct, winnowing the bottom

And the shoulders of one prepubescent
– She of the bubble machine. Even those unlisted
Still should readily appreciate

Her tight, smooth, priceless presence here.
Bubbles she catches he pinches she scratches,
Leaving Mum to *Whisper of the Living*.

Smell of Rape

The honeysuckle is about to flower
And delicate things are come across under the beeches.
If you hunker down, you may glimpse them.
They've a whole forest to explore to the west of the M11.
Tulips black as night would please Dumas
Were he to visit my Tottenham garden this year,
While that magnolia I've still to plant
Gets knocked about. I'll do it this weekend.
Already the kitchen's been given its seasonal mop,
While sprinklers form rainbows and provide a backdrop
To those who glide past beds on roller-blades.
Bluebells mist the grounds of Kew, though it's now
Almost clear enough to glimpse the sea
From Inkpen Beacon. And it's a new tax year.
Don't forget to put those bills from before
Into their own envelope. It's time to weed the
Allotment, empty your hoary old pots
Or to retire with a pal to some hideout known
Only to kids while others get on with the pruning,
The paint-jobs, the sales. Gran's Toyota
Needs a good shampooing. Some of her knock-kneed
Knick-knacks plead to be sold off via the car boot.
It's now warm enough to sample the night air
With your shoulders bare after dancing
Or sit in the sun, guzzling oysters
And washing them down with champagne.
Take two cows, Taffy, croons the woodland to the thief,
With all the twigs and Daphne
Herself reaching up and bursting into leaf.

A Seat for a Sage

Sometimes I can't find it or perhaps
It isn't in its usual place, deep in the forest's heart.
It's where I like to take the latest girl,

So if it isn't there it can put me out of my stride,
As it were. But when we manage
To reach it I am pleased and sit there

On the throne that's grown for me
Between its serpent roots. And she may take
A picture, which I won't bury with her

Underneath the beech nuts that I strew
Over her last bed, leaving not the slightest
Clue as to her whereabouts. Would you?

Instead I post it on Facebook for my Buddhist pals:
Their meditation's verdant inspiration,
While the search continues somewhere else.

Epping Forest

Drum Country

The mud on the ground, at a sudden stop to the road,
Does tractor impressions, then the wire runs taut
And barbed along those concrete, hockey-stick bowed
Posts overhanging their mesh, keeping us out
Of the Ministry's place, the land of the white cloud.

Sporadic puffs and vapours fume from the lips
Of chimneys there, beyond some flattish meadows
Where patchy cattle graze in front of heaps
Of puce clinker – cattle brushed by shadows
Clouds cast over them while they nose the buttercups.

That realm of pipes and rails all shades of rust
Projects faint sirens even as the nightingale
Jugs it in a thorn bush, just where the ditch is lost
In willow-herb and rushes. Humming cables trail
From lofty masts of pylons over rushes flowing east.

There's a metal taste to the air, and yet the sky
Is one wide bowl of space where cirrus melts.
Robbed of bark, a tree-hulk shines nearby,
Stark against a silhouette of catwalks and conveyor-belts
Knocked blotto by the lift-off, as wild duck let fly

Cacophonies of flap! Outstretching fate,
They veer before the herd which turns to look,
Which blows, but then crops on without debate
Near willow-sheltered reeds beside a brook
At the meadow's corner, close to a five-bar gate.

Jaguar Country

Towards the end of autumn, sleek as a motorway hawk,
It cruised past me on my way up to Leamington.
There I'd find *my* habitat underneath a duvet.
She was partial to Land Rovers, and to one last walk.

The mistletoe was in evidence through twigs,
While far off thorns divided plough from fallow.
The grey hazed. Intensifying ochres
Blazed against evergreens in the park across a bridge

Of Cotswold stone guarded by sphinxes. Gryphons
Flanked the steps leading into the arboretum
From a parterre whose pattern might only be appreciated
In a negligee, through the panes of a five-star bedroom.

Wellingtonias, yews, and then one brilliant yellow mass
On from the site once Peugeot – I spied light on water
After we had glimpsed those spotted woodpeckers.
Gleams flashed on each ripple. Leaves would shower

Suddenly. A branch waved like a ribbon beyond some
Bulrush sentinel. Herons adhered to one-upmanship
On the highest branches of their isle. We never managed
To sight the deer nor inspect that vintage E-type

Last year in a lobby. And there had to be
A lane we missed that led into some parded wood
Darker than any tramped through that weekend
When lava flowed me home through canyons of obscurity.

Esturial Philosophy

Bristling teasels here grow upright, brandished
On barbed forks, where otherwise almost everything
Inclines towards the horizontal. After a last firm ridge,
The coastline melts away while shallow pools
And squidgy, cormorant-frequented mudflats
Stretch ahead till blocked; stopped by groynes
Partitioning the tidal shore of a river open to a sea
That's out as often as it's in.
                             And here we are,
On one side of it, seeking views of this brown god
Who sprawls among his little ports, seaside towns
With bathing-huts, garish piers at faltering resorts,
Cafés draped in fishing net and marshes
And promontories like this one. Not a house in sight:
One long, lagoony curve bordered by
Track-threaded wilderness veering away from us
Into the haze.
                Across the sizeable inlet ahead,
There is the suggestion of a country not entirely of this earth;
A landscape rendered mythical by atmosphere,
Sparingly affording us the tantalising outline
Of a panorama ordinary enough but more pastoral
Than ours can ever be: a half-dreamt territory
The overweight person enlarging from the ankles
In extraordinary chequered trousers ambles towards,
Between thistles and teasels.
                    He kicks things with a toe,
Picks up items and then casts them aside,
As he and a slight companion go ahead of us,

Diminishing, claimed by distance, as by lack of interest:
People we shall never see again, as with most of our
    fellow men;
Who have no more business with us than we with them
And vanish beneath a sedately lowering sun.

Seeing Myself

He'd like to get his stones to skip across …
And there has been a boy here doing this
As long as there have been boys, I guess.

The sea flicks its unsettled fringes at us
And there is this flick something back at it,
Skim neat stones over its undulant nap.

You have to choose the right sort of stones
Less than a stone's throw from the shore,
Used by the sea already, those that fit.

4
Beachcomber

RIO DE JANEIRO

Tristeza

That pensive spell, the sadness that you see
In Gauguin's women, for instance, sitting quietly,
A faraway look in their eyes, as if deep
In melancholy thought – it's not: it's the heat,
And the way the heat comes back, that brooding gaze,
Abstracted, prompting such words as 'lointain',
Yet there is something sad about heat – it wells up at noon,
Prompting you to choose the shaded side of the avenue
And placing a value on *sombra* rather than *sol*.
The Romans knew that ghosts appear at midday
In the haze as it wobbles up from the ground,
And as for Brazil it is under that spell
Brewed by the tropics, inducing a trance
Moved by the minor key of the Bossa Nova.

Evening

I look down onto the trees that hide the light,
Eight floors below, on Siqueira Campos Street.
A roof slides by beneath the spreading leaves.
We keep our doors ajar to tempt a breeze,
Using a sandal perhaps as a door-stop.

Most of my view is the fifteen floors of a car-park;
But above the adjacent building there's a crag
Craning up out of the bush that laps at the back
Of the flats, and between that block and the next
There's a single palm, dishevelled, thin

And very tall, but not of sufficient height
To match the blocks on Siqueira Campos Street
Where one may find the very thing one seeks
Under my room, in the market of antiques.
Needing a break, I lean out, taking in verticals:

Variant sets of balconies, shutters and windows.
The day has passed in a whirl, and a fan
Keeps turning over there, and further along a girl
Is stroking her hair, looking out in a dream, like me,
With everything else in darkness, except for her tv.

How to Lose Your Job

The girl from Ipanema
Swings down the Avenida
Humming to herself
The Girl from Ipanema.

The boy handing out slips,
One foot up the wall,
Deep in some reading material,
Doesn't see her at all.

The Forbidden Rose

Her outline may undulate according to the hills,
But her navel is the target when I glance:
It's in a hollow framed by the wings of her hips,
As she lies on her side, reading a romance.

The fingers of her free hand make contact
With her body here and there, brushing off
Grains, adjusting her top, ravelling her hair.

She's a bit like a pony, whisking its tail
While grazing as intently as she reads.
Once only, she pauses, to reach for the nape
Of her lover, who rests on an elbow

Behind her, baring her throat to him
As the sea sends in its horses, annexes the beach
And withdraws, then it's back to her book.

Waiting

A large policeman mounted on a motorbike
Gets his diminutive partner to give him a push.
To no avail – they make ignominious progress
Across the intersection. The bike refuses to roar
Into life, just as the rain refuses to come down.
Everyone is beginning to complain, and the sky
Goes dark, but the clouds are just not
Ready to burst, and pretty soon the heavens
Are empty again. It's close to carnival time,
When everyone is supposed to let their hair down.
The blast of chill air from the bank is more
Than cancelled out by simmering traffic.
Things with exoskeletons do well.
The cockroaches are positively bustling.
Humans lie prone on flattened sheets of cardboard.
The stones are slicked with dirt, and the air
Is full of dust. It must rain. It must.
But it doesn't. Every dove has turned into a pigeon.
As for the women, rather than share their beds
They prefer to sleep on the floor. There's no breeze at all,
And the trees are so still they could be a painting,
The dogs look dead except for their panting,
The canaries are all fainting, and only some rain
Will ease the situation, wash the streets clean,
And with its downpour drench the night in sperm.

Airborne

The butterfly that fluttered through the carnival
Didn't wear a costume. Why should it have?
Its wings were the colour of rust
And featured a fair spattering of polka-dots.

Its flight, about which there was something frantic,
Was only to be seen intermittently, between
The haunches of a gorilla and the legs
Of a female marine. How unlike the vultures

Over the favela, that evening we sat
On its brow. Vultures above and below,
Wings outspread to the very last feather,
Gliding with motionless ease ...

The Model

A halberd leans against the wall.
It says, in effect, a peasant with a skill
Can bring down a prince
(Charles the Bold, for instance).
This thorny axe may signify
The carnage that was Paraguay,
But then it also stands for ceremonial.
Debret's young chap arrives at court in Brazil
With a fine cocked hat and a parasol
Followed by his black,
Her arms full of his gear,
Including the weapon shown here.

Our painter hails from the boon dogs though.
You can tell it by his beard.
He has just rolled himself a cigarette,
And is sharing a joke with the girl who is on her break
And at his upright, fingering a tune.
From the waist down, she's wrapped in a shawl,
So he gets the front of the lass
While we get to peek at her naked back.

As back-views go, it's far from academic.
His studio in Montparnasse
Is chock-a-block with props,
But what the room is full of is her smile.

*'The Model on Her Break' by Almeida Júnior, Brazilian artist,
1850–99*

In Praise of Shopping

Indigenous people from isolated communities, perhaps on the banks
   of some tributary of the Amazon, always consume what they
   catch.
So they can be nonplussed by the constant availability of everything
   all of the time – what is one meant to do?
Eat until one bursts, dress until one suffocates?
Of course it feels morally right not to possess something you very
   clearly need, since then you can hunt for it without guilt.
However, this demotes the act to the ranks of the merely functional.
To give your shopping flavour, guilt is an obligatory seasoning.
The purest spirit is best expressed when one is out unnecessarily,
   looking for some item you may never use.
Even then it has benefits: to say it's therapeutic is a cliché,
   but it's not just loneliness that it heals.
Shopping can be used as an antidote to Alzheimer's: you have
   to remember where the shop is, and whether you have already
   bought the item.
So long as one's card accepts one, a purchase is always an
   affirmation.
Buying via the internet is neither as rewarding nor as complex
   as handing your card to one of the opposite sex.
Shoppers express the fundamental characteristics of their make-up:
   my son likes designer labels, and snuggled his mum's when he
   sucked his thumb.
I am more partial to a bargain: exhibiting a taste for the low-life,
   I grub through unsavoury piles in charity stores created for the
   homeless.
I'm always looking for two for the price of one, perhaps because
   I'm a single mother's son.

I am also an inveterate collector, so if I reach Nirvana
    I will find it filled with cut-price CDs, second-hand t-shirts
    and remaindered books.
But I also like to wander in the presence of up-market shops.
It's flattering how each offers me its well-appointed wares –
    of course the very finest are discreet.
Steeped in the poetry of boutiques, I can lie awake like a girl
    at night, reciting their names instead of sheep.
What problems I'd have if I were a girl! Searching for cut-price
    manicures, second hand hair-dos and remaindered
    magazines.
I have been known to buy negligées 'just in case'.
Not in case I turn into one, but in case I ever again get one
    to buy things for: bras, panties, shoes, earrings,
    anything wearable but not too practical – I've seldom
    got it right with a tampon.
Shopping in the heat favours the shaded side, stone arcades,
    air-conditioning, comprehensive stores.
Chunks of chilled air tempt one to abandon the pavement
    as if the doors were extending invitations.
Others open wide on their own, simply upon sensing an
    approach.
When I was young and well-formed, women used to do that
    for me.

The Mother

I am sitting on a rock beside the sea.
My newborn tugs at my nipple.
He feels new to me, and yet
I have carried him everywhere
Since he began. He is still
Something of a stranger, but he is a man.
The gift of his father to me.
We have come here to be naked
By this awe-inspiring sea.
I am addicted to men.
Men who are strong and quick
In thought and deed. Men who are gods
To their sons and daughters;
Who teach them bike and ball control.
I am in love with my man.
I don't want the others to lie with me.
But I do like to watch as they move around.
Men who are basically sound.
Men who maintain and move big cranes,
Men with large hands,
Wearing hard hats at work,
But here today, beautiful and free.
Not to be dismissed, their qualities of strength,
Speed and skill: that overhead goal,
And the way a guy moved to snatch a small boy
Out of the blur of the traffic.

Sweat

Switch from the metro maintained by ice-girls
To the platform which is not and your pores
Start to react, as they do up the flights
To the third floor dance under fans
Old enough to be offered a seat
If they were using the metro.

Work up a sweat on the beach with a ball,
Wake up drenched in it in the small hours
Or get through several t-shirts on a good
Stiff scramble through semi-vertical
And sub-tropical forest up to some lookout.
Yes, but you also work up a lather
Choosing a t-shirt on the Avenue
Of Our Lady of Copacabana.

Be aware that this is recreational.
When it accompanies loading
Pieces from some concrete jigsaw
Into a chute placed above a skip …
Now you get it! Stepping around
Some works into oncoming cars.

Measure each bollard, polished tile
Or piece of pavement mosaic
Kicked out of place in pints of it.

Acai

I think vanity has had a bad press.
I'd say it's good for you, more or less.
Vanity keeps you at a decent weight.
When you see a 60 year old with a 6-pack,
You can put it down to Vanity.
Vanity sustains the fitness industry.
A special joggers' and cyclists' path
Runs alongside the promenades.
There are open-air gyms with shiny bars
And you can improve beneath the stars.
Arpoador beach has an outdoor gym
Overlooking the sand beyond the headland.
The weights are concrete and the bars rusted.
But people train in the rain.
They train because they are vain –
But you can look at them again and again.
Vanity is responsible for all this.
For girls wearing t-shirts which say YOGA,
Thrusting the word out at you.
Beautiful! Vanity improves.
I don't understand why it's considered a vice.
People who are fit feel nice.
Vanity is justified.
It should be beatified.
What a packed place of worship that would be!
A temple, dedicated to vanity.
Vanity demands you stay healthy.

That is why there's a juice bar on every corner,
With every sort of juice, including
About seven no European has ever heard of.
Best of all is a giant cup of frozen black sludge.
Too many spoonfuls too fast,
And you get a head-ache –
Gives you a great complexion though,
And if you are going to wear a bikini
That's just a few pieces of string,
Bear in mind it's not the thing
We're looking at, it's you,
And that part you can't even see in a mirror.
Pamper it with aloe vera.
Vanity demands you do.
Beware of preachers spouting tripe,
And while you can, stay smooth and ripe.

The Armourer's Wife

Not long after her wedding day,
While she's on her honeymoon perhaps,
I watch her on the beach, at play,
And fall into her traps …
I could be the foam, or I could be
That grain of sand

On her inner thigh, and then,
When the wave knocks her down
And bowls her over and along,
The sand gets up inside her thong,
And I could be there, or be the air
Breathing on her, freshening her hair.

I could be an earring in her ear
And pass right through the lobe.
I could be her Coke or her Sprite.
An Arab song gets belted out
And she does a dance with her towel.
I could be that.

She lifts and lowers a hip.
People start to clap,
And now a lanky young geek
Wants her for his mobile phone.
I'd rate her for her bum alone
With its butterfly inked on a cheek.

Existence

The red flag tugs at its pole in front of the Mar;
The Windsor's welcoming mat demands to be swept;
Guests favour the pool at the Othon over the beach,
While who booked a manicure stews in the Palace bar.

Blown into wrinkles, the sea is mass of glissades.
When a wave breaks its spume gets flung to the South.
My paperback flicks frenziedly through its own pages.
I have no means of escape from the sand's fusillades.

Open-air showers go flaring along the horizon;
Pigeons get pummelled, seabirds grapple the clouds;
The palms are engaged in a Dionysian revel,
While kites that are bats get into a sinister flap.

Whatever is free or has ends or loose covers vibrates.
Floppy hats, inflatables and parasols get bowled away.
Only the ponderous bulk of a JCB
Seems unaffected, while the shore trembles beneath me

As it impresses the sand with its ongoing treads
To which the surf is indifferent, rubbing these out
With a practised swipe, as the wind persists in its mission
Of wiping the rootless off this ephemeral map.

Ode to the Sunset

It's a February evening. The liners leaving port
Are still in the sun. They gleam on the horizon
Between this beach's bow and the northern peaks.
Here, the sun's just set behind the Marriot,
But no one seems to want to leave just yet.
Long, lazy waves keep rolling in, neither too rough
Nor too gentle, at the end of a baking day.

It's lilac out at sea, while a crag behind the front
Is gilded by our burning star, its crown of trees
Picked out against a final beige and cerise.
People are still at play, racing in or wading out
Or rolling about or going head-first into surges,
To surface, adjusting their cossies. Others stroll
Along the slick, wet edge, or simply sit and watch.

Nobody sneers at the sea. None of us seem
To have a problem with it as we may with art.
It seems better than tv – more honestly
Always the same and ever changing. Now
The eastern sky has a rose pink hue,
But nobody seems prepared to go.
It's Sunday. They want to spin it out.

They want to mark the waves as they build,
And as they fall, or look at other people:
What they do, how they're built, who they have
The hots for. The crag darkens. A kite in silhouette
Nibbles at its sheer edge, and on the palmy roofs
Of the penthouses, millionaires and minas
Can be imagined sinking caipirinhas.

The sea darkens, green by now only where the waves
Achieve their critical mass and over-bend.
There are still some of us out bathing though
Since nobody wants this day to end,
But the moon has appeared, half-submerged,
If crisp as can be in its own part of the sky
Where the great birds float, incredibly high.

The vendors have already gone away,
And the promenade's been lit, its condos black
Against a deepening red. People
Start to leave at last, reluctantly, as the moon
Begins to shine, brightening with every passing minute.
What ships go forth are nests of light,
And only the breaking surf defies the night.

Grumarí

The leaves
      hardly breathe
           and snakes
      loop round
the branches,
      soaking up heat
           from cars parked
      nose to tail
outside
      the seafood
           kiosk by
      this savage
southern
      beach where
the leaves
      hardly breathe
           and snakes
      loop round
the branches,
      soaking up heat
           from cars parked
      nose to tail
outside
      the seafood
           kiosk by
      this savage
southern
      beach.